Short Walks in

Hadrians Wall Country

Terry Dixon

Acknowledgements

We all owe a great debt to the countless number of people who have created and maintained the footpaths which allow us easy access into some of the most beautiful parts of the country.

The route maps included in this guide are based on the 1:25000 Ordnance Survey Pathfinder series, with the permission of The Controller of HMSO.

My thanks to **Family and Friends** who have walked these paths over the years and helped check them out.

Tourist Information Centres

Bellingham	Main Street.	01434 220616
Brampton	Moot Hall, Market Place.	016977 3433
Corbridge	Hill Street. (seasonal	01434 632815
Haltwhistle	Church Hall, Main Street.	01434 322002
Hexham	**The Manor Office, Hallgate.**	**01434 605225**
Once Brewed	Military Road, Bardon Mill.	01434 344396
Prudhoe	Waterworld, Front Street.	01661 833144

While every care has been taken to ensure that the text is accurate and upto date, the publisher cannot accept any responsibility for errors or inaccuracies. Changes in the form of diversions, renewed stiles or bridges etc. occur continuously in the countryside and may affect the walks in places. The paths which these walks follow, however, are generally on recognised 'rights of way' and in many cases have been in existence for generations. They have all been checked recently and as many are well signposted by the National Parks Authority, surprises should be relatively few.

Contents

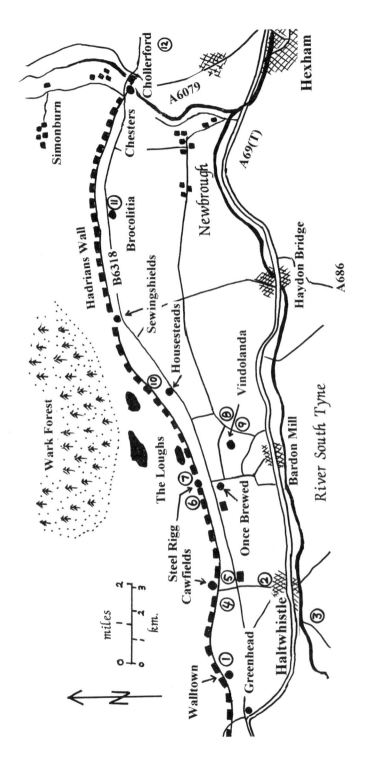

Location of the Walks

Introduction

Stretching across the northern slopes of the Tyne valley, Hadrians Wall traverses some of the wildest and most beautiful countryside in Northumberland. An exhillerating walk along the Whinsill ridge on a clear day will give panoramic views of the Cheviots to the north, the Pennines to the south and the peaks of the Lake District fifty miles to the south-west. From Windshield Crags, the highest point, the rise and fall of the Whinsill continues uninterrupted in both directions, and the majestic ridges are capped, more often than not, by the magnetic attraction of Hadrians Wall.

Each walk descripion is accompanied by a simple outline map detailing the relevant features of the route. The description is detailed only where necessary, and together with the maps should be quite sufficient to get you round the walks with the minimum of fuss.

Basic Assumptions

These walk descriptions are offered with a few basic assumptions.

While out walking, safety is an individual responsibility. It is always advisable to check the local weather forecast, take a map and know how to use it. The 0rdnance Survey Pathfinder is an excellent map with a considerable amount of fine detail, and although not absolutely neccessary for walks of this nature *you are recommended to carry at least a copy of the O.S. Landranger sheet number 87*, a 1:50000 scale map, which covers most of the area.

Circumstances change rapidly in foul weather conditions, and it is wise, as the scouts say, to *'Be Prepared'*.

The publisher cannot be held responsible for errors or omissions in the text and it is often the case that a common sense approach, rather than a slavish obedience to text, is the best way forward.

The countryside is worthy of respect. While enjoying its beauty please observe the country code, and encourage others to do likewise.

5

Refreshments on Route

Walk

1. Holmhead, a small guest house in the shadow of Thirlwall Castle, and right on the route, offers light refreshments.
2. The town of Haltwhistle borders the walk, but if you prefer a country pub, try the Milecastle Inn up on the Military road.
3. Either Haltwhistle, or the Wallace Arms at Rowfoot.

4/5. The Milecastle on the main road, or, occasionally, a refreshments caravan at Cawfields.

6/7. The Twice Brewed Inn on the main road, or, The Vallum Restaurant a short distance further west.

8/9. Vindolanda/Chesterholme provides light refreshments, and Bardon mill is fairly close to the walk.

8/10. A small kiosk at the Housesteads car park provides the basics.

11. Nothing at Brocolitia, but a small cafe at Simonburn.

On Four Legs

Some of these walks are quite suitable for dogs, particularly those without too many stiles as these tend to prove not too popular with our four-legged friends. Perhaps it is the poor owner who is much more likely to suffer as we lift them bodily over. A careful look at the enclosed maps should save you the embarrassment of paw marks or mud all over your new anorak or, even worse, a strained back. Haltwhistle Burn, the walk at Bellister, and Chineley Burn probably provide the fewest obstacles. The walk along the wall is also worth considering, but the crags are close at hand. Do remember, above all else, that this is a farming area with a fair number of sheep on the fells.

Transport

Getting to the start point of these walks is possible using public transport. The walks which start at Haltwhistle are very close to the main line services provided by both rail and bus routes, however the others depend upon a choice of bus services which are seasonal and do vary in frequency for Sunday travel.

People travelling from outside the area can use the normal transport network to Haltwhistle or Hexham, and from these towns will need to use the **Hadrians Wall Bus Service** which links most of the major sites of interest and, apart from the walks at Simonburn and Fallowfield, the start points of many wonderful walks. These services are supported by various public bodies, and are known as the Hadrians Wall Bus East when leaving from Hexham and the Hadrians Wall Bus West when leaving Carlisle. As well as overlapping along the popular areas between Greenhead and Vindolanda they also connect with the main train service through the Tyne gap between Carlisle and Newcastle.

There is a colourful and informative leaflet giving full details of the Hadrians Wall Bus service, including times, fares and a list of useful phone numbers. Special mention is made of the bargain whole day **Rover ticket,** ideal for those who wish to arrange a linear walk or perhaps want to visit a selection of sites. An ideal park and ride, particularly during the summer months when the sevice is at its best.

Enquiries:- Bus East   01434-605555/605225
           West   01228-812812

The **purpose built carparks and amenity areas** at the most popular locations such as Walltown, Cawfields, Steel Rigg, Vindolanda and Housesteads are excellent start points for many delightful walks, but inevitably tend to be busy at peak periods with some of the problems of city carparks.

Walltown(GR. NY668660) The quarry first opened just over one hundred years ago to produce paving stones and extract Whinstone for roadmaking, and resulted, like Cawfields, in the destruction of large sections of wall. One such sudden end can be clearly seen at Walltown Crags. The National Parks have developed the site to provide an information point with a Park warden on a seasonal basis, parking and toilet facilities.

Cawfields Quarry(GR. NY713666). Created by the National Parks in 1974, this site provides an excellent starting point for several walks, two of which are described in this guide. The walk to the west, along the ridge towards Walltown, is spectacular with fabulous views in all directions. Likewise, going eastbound, the path goes along Cawfield Crags and returns at a lower level. With the lake and rock face nearby, Cawfields is an attractive site, but the quarrying in this area which continued until a few decades ago destroyed a whole section of the wall. The rock face which has been left exposed is a section through the Great Whinsill, with the scarp and dip slopes being quite distinctive.

Steel Rigg(GR. NY751677) No facilities, but an excellent starting point with fabulous views of the crags.

Vindolanda(GR. NY769664) There are two carparks here on the line of the Stanegate, both of which serve this famous Roman site and museum. They are also handy start points for two of the walks described. The eastern car park is at GR. NY774665

Housesteads(GR. NY794684) Large parking area at the side of the 'Military' road, with refreshments, toilet facilities, shop and information. Situated about ten minutes walk from the fort itself.

Brocolitia (NY858710) is situated in a raw and exposed area on the moorland. A stones throw from the carpark lies a replica of the Mithraic temple, and a short distance to the north of the temple a marshy hollow marks the spot of Coventinas Well, a shrine from which came one of the best caches of Roman coins found in the area.

These car parks can all be found on the O.S. Pathfinder series, Maps 546 (NY66/76), and 534 (87/97), and all walks in this book are located on the **NY** section of the Ordnance Survey

Using this Guide

To help you use and get the best from this guide, the text and maps, where possible, are uniform throughout. Each walk is relatively easy, and is graded simply by the time taken to complete it by an average healthy adult, and, a reasonably keen five year old. Indication is given under the heading section of any relevant information including difficulties or elements of risk, for example :-

Heading	Information	Explanation
Distance	5 miles/8km.	rounded to nearest ¼ mile/km.
Time	1½ - 2 hours	adult time - children's time
Ascent	200ft/60m.	rounded to nearest 50 ft/10m.
Maps	L87, P546/547	Landranger or Pathfinder
Caution	undercut riverbank	indicated on map
Start	Position	Description

Symbols used

START	Start	Ⓢ	Alternative start
↗	Orientation, Map North	x ?	Caution
Ⓒ	Cafe or Restaurant	+	Church
PH	Public House	T	Telephone
P	Car park, official	Ⓟ	Car park, roadside
▪ □	Buildings	///,	Built up area
⅍	Bridge over river	⋈	River ford
=	Road, fenced or walled	_ _ ⁻	Footpath
⁓⁓⁓	Road, unfenced or bridleway	S	Stile
G	Gate	▲	Triangulation point
♠	Coniferous woodland	♠	Deciduous woodland
♠♠	Mixed woodland	▬▬	Line of Hadrians Wall

General Notes

When planning your route there are various ways of assessing how long it will take you. These walks have been repeated many times however, and from experience the time allowed should give a healthy but not particularly fit adult, together with a keen five year old, plenty of time to stroll around the walk. No two adults or children are alike, but the times given are fairly realistic. You will of course need to add time for stops, picnics, pictures etc.

Objective dangers are relatively few, but where appropriate are mentioned in the text and on the maps as (?) or (X). It is wise to keep to the footpaths, particularly along the cliffs of the Whinsill, but also in the various denes where mining remains may prove hazardous to the unwary or careless. Children, of course, love these areas, and extra vigilance is essential.

Isolation on these routes is generally not a great problem during the summer months, however weather conditions can change rapidly and during off-peak periods you may be surprised to find fewer walkers on the hill than expected.

Enjoy the countryside and respect its life and work
Keep your dogs under close control
Keep to public paths across farmland
Guard against all risk of fire
Fasten all gates
Use gates and stiles to cross fences, hedges and walls
Take your litter home
Leave livestock, crops and machinery alone
Help to keep all water clean
Protect wildlife, plants and trees
Take special care on country roads
Make no unnecessary noise

1   Walltown & Thirlwall castle

A very satisfying walk with lots of variety. The route goes via Walltown Crags, Cairny Croft, the Tipalt Burn, Thirlwall Castle and finally along the Roman fighting ditch to within a stones throw of the Roman Army Museum at Carvoran which is well worth a visit.

Distance	4miles(6$^1/_2$km)
Time	2-2$^1/_2$hrs.
Ascent	400ft(120m)
Maps	Landranger 87, Pathfinder 546(NY66/76)
Caution	One of the larger carparks in the area, although not quite as isolated as Steel Rigg or Cawfields.
Start	Walltown carpark, lies about five minutes, by car, north-east of Greenhead. From this village follow the Military Road up the hill until the signposts direct you to the museum. The carpark is just past the entrance. The walk may also start from Greenhead or perhaps the hamlet of Holmhead near the castle. GR. NY668660

1.   From the carpark, just a few yards south of the entrance, a signpost directs you along a path which passes behind the stone-built National Parks building. This is part of the Pennine Way and it parallels the road up to Walltown. Initially, directly behind the carpark through woods, the track rises to give good views across the quarried area. An information board here gives most of the route in outline form, together with information in several languages. The quarrying enterprise of the last hundred years, although now providing a good parking and amenity area, has destroyed large tracts of the Whinsill, and this can be seen quite clearly as the walk approaches Walltown. Follow the path as it hugs the roadside, and then on the road itself to another much smaller parking area. At this point strike up the slope on the left at right angles to reach Walltown

crags. The wall here is in very good shape and looks particularly impressive in the dip to the left. Once on the ridge turn right. The going is nice and easy, although a brisk westerly wind could easily change that. Note where the wall comes to an abrupt halt at the edge of the quarried cliff. After ten minutes stroll in the steps of the Romans, the farm appears and then a steep descent into Walltown Nick. Legend has it that King Arthurs well, a small spring which lies hereabouts, was used to baptise King Egbert and his retinue in AD627.

2.   The wall, of course, continues straight ahead here, and it is very tempting to do just that. Perhaps another day! Turn left along the wide stony track, zig-zagging across a permanent area of mudbath concentrated around two old stone gateposts. Go half left heading for the ladder stile a few hundred paces distant. There is sometimes a bull in this section of rough pasture, but with all the other animals around there is little chance of attracting more than a flicker of interest - So I am informed! After crossing the stile, the descent crosses a footbridge and then up to the tarmac lane. On the descent take a look across to the left. The rock outcrop, from a certain angle, takes on the shape of a face in profile.

3.   Turn left down the lane. To shorten the walk just continue for about twenty minutes and this will take you directly back to the carpark. The planned route, however, takes the first right towards, and then around, High Old Shield Farm via three stiles. The way is well marked with two more stiles on the way down to the Tipalt Burn. The second of these is concealed by the slope of the land. Immediately after this bear left towards another stile and, yes, a signpost. Continue past the sign to a broken down wall, more like a mound really, which crosses the path. If you take the right turn here and stroll easily down to the burn, you will find an idyllic setting near the waters

12

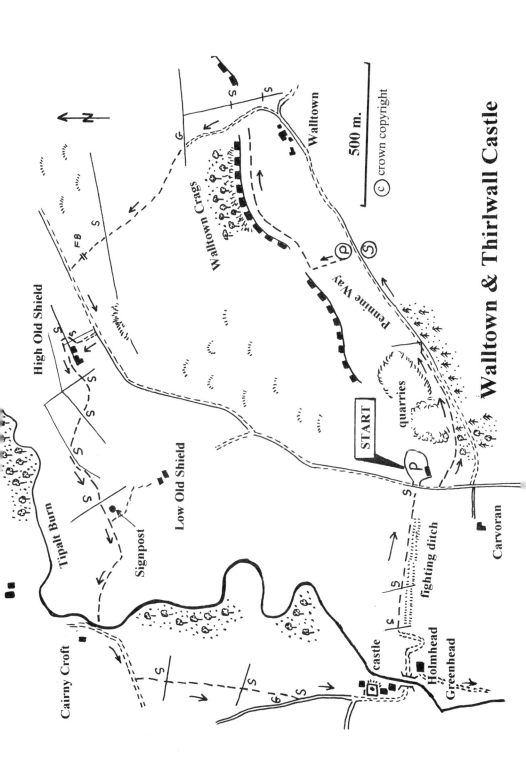

Walltown & Thirlwall Castle

© crown copyright

500 m.

N

Walltown

Walltown Crags

Pennine Way

quarries

START

Carvoran

High Old Shield

Tipalt Burn

Low Old Shield

Signpost

Cairny Croft

castle

Holmhead

Greenhead

fighting ditch

edge, with the croft sitting high on the opposite bank. The stream disappears into the steep sided vegetation choked gulley on the left, but our way follows the stepping stones over the burn.

4. Follow the tarmac up to the left towards a house, looking for a stile on the left hand side. The lush pasture is crossed, going slightly right, using two more stiles until the road is reached via a gate or stone stile set into the wall on the left. Just down the lane on the left is Thirwall Castle with its impressive south-west wall standing proudly above the earth mound. Continue through a metal gate and walk in front of the castle. Two signposts mark the different directions of

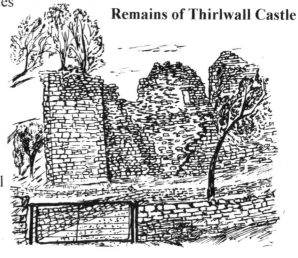

Remains of Thirlwall Castle

the Pennine Way. Take the left hand one and this will lead you to the footbridge over the stream at Holmhead. This is a charming and well concealed little hamlet in the shadow of the castle and is well worth a stop. The large house on the right over the bridge is primarily a B&B, but tea and snacks are available and hikers are made most welcome.

5. The last stretch is uphill so make the most of your teabreak. Continue along the lane, bearing left, and follow it uphill as it zig-zags towards a gate and finger post. The pasture beyond slopes fairly easily and the prominent Roman 'fighting ditch' can be followed ahead to the skyline, crossing a couple of walls on the way up. Soon the buildings of the Roman Army Museum come into view on the right, and you should now be in a position to see the full panorama with good views in all directions. Continue downhill, and all too soon the starting point lies just ahead on the other side of the road.

14

2   Haltwhistle Burn & Hallpeatmoss

An interesting mixed walk combining the delights of easy walking on good paths up the side of Haltwhistle Burn and the almost level moorland around Hallpeatmoss. The start point can be one of two locations in Haltwhistle, or the Milecastle Inn on the Military Road.

Distance	4miles(6$^1{}_2$km)
Time	2 - 2 $^1/_2$ hours
Ascent	400 ft(120m)
Maps	Landranger 88, Pathfinder 546 (NY 66/76)
Caution	Old mine workings along the burn and shafts on the moors always need care.
Start	Several good points. The walk is described from the public car park at Walter Willsons, the supermarket in Haltwhistle. G.R.707642. The Milecastle Inn at G.R.716660 is an equally good place to start, with obvious advantages at the end of the walk, as indeed is the bridge at Townfoot G.R. 713642

---

1.   From the carpark, cross the road, bearing left until you can turn right into Willea Road. This street leads to the Haltwhistle Burn itself, passing a gravel parking area on the right before curving left to parallel the burn where it passes the old clayworks. At this point a 'weak bridge' can be used to cross the stream. Presumably weak for commercial vehicles rather than the odd walker, but if any doubts linger a footbridge five minutes along the road will serve the same pupose,and the walk can be joined at that point.

2.   Once over the bridge we turn left to follow the river bank and soon a bench seat appears in a tranquil setting facing the burn, a

memorial to Harry Miller the Town Clerk of Haltwhistle. The burn begins its life much further north in the peat hags beyond Hadrians Wall. As the Caw Burn, it flows southwards having gouged it's way through the whinsill at Caw Gap and then, with a quick name change, continues the short journey down to join the South Tyne. Cutting its way through the strata it has left craggy outcrops at intervals along the valley sides, and now passes a rich mixture of the local industrial heritage which has risen and fallen in the last few hundred years. The walk at this point follows the old mineral line. Nearby a path crosses our way. On the left a bridge gives access to the previously mentioned tarmac road and on our right the sign directs the way to the 'Doors', a farm which can be found near the Milecastle Inn. Continue along the main path to an open area complete with a picnic table. Several more gates, bridges and seats follow before the valley opens out close to the Military Road, and also a few items of industrial history which somehow seem to blend in with the this picturesque little valley.

You will not miss the chimney off on the right, nor the foundations of the old engine house. These are all that remain now of the secondary entrance to the South Tyne Colliery whose main shaft was further down the valley. Watch out for the numerous prominent vertical bolts which, projecting out of the grassed area, are just waiting for the careless. Further on, the remains of old lime kilns can be seen on both sides of the burn, built to take advantage of the two most important ingredients of quicklime, coal and limestone, which were found together in this area. Looking over your shoulder the farm buildings of Lees Hall sit high above the stream on the side of the fell. Over the last footbridge and follow the grassy path up leftwards to the field corner where a gate leads on to the Military Road. Turn

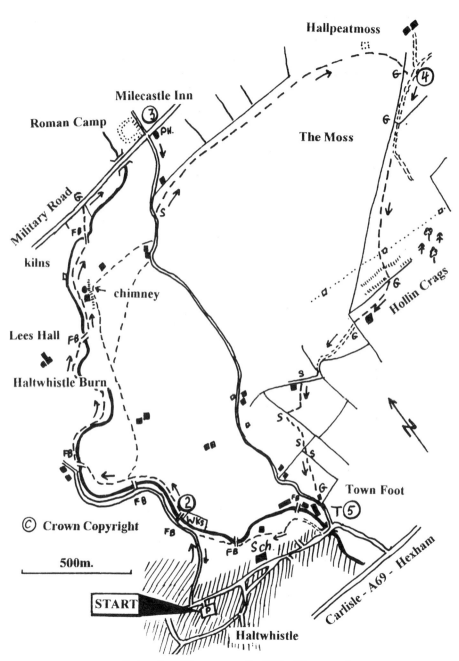

Hallpeatmoss

The Moss

Milecastle Inn
Roman Camp
③
PH.
S

Military Road
G
FB
kilns
chimney
S

G
Hollin Crags

④
G
G

Lees Hall FB
Haltwhistle Burn

s
S

© Crown Copyright
S
S

FB
Town Foot
G
T ⑤

FB
②
(WKS)
FB
Sch.

500m.

START
Haltwhistle
Carlisle - A69 - Hexham

Haltwhistle Burn & Hallpeatmoss

right and head for the Inn which lies a few hundred metres away. The road is fast and furious, so take care.

3.   The Milecastle Inn might well be a good place to start and finish the walk. Perhaps the time of day or evening is the critical factor!

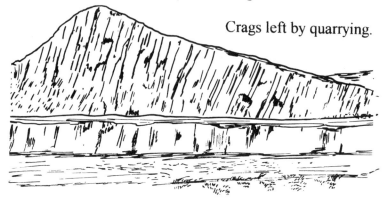

Crags left by quarrying.

Take the tarmac road to the right, going uphill and southbound, past a house, and then left at a stile with a sign 'Hallpeatmoss 1 mile'. The going is nice and easy, almost flat in places, although tussocky and undulating if you stray off the path. Perhaps the plural 'paths' would be more appropriate, because there are at least two. The lefthand one, nearest the wall, is better, and as well as being more enduring it puts you in a position closer to the mini ridge where it is possible to see the Whinsill stretching miles away to the east. The crag, which was part of Cawfields Quarry, can just be seen away to the north, and it was from here that whinsill was cut and transported to Haltwhistle via the mineral line which we followed on our journey up the burn. Ahead of us, the farm at Hallpeat Moss comes into view sitting below the next hill. For years it was the property of the Ridley family, and the name is said to be derived from ' the place where peat was cut for the hall '. As we leave the wall behind us we need to bear right slightly as the ground descends. Just ahead there is an area of bog and reeds, fenced off to prevent the animals getting into difficulty. Keep this to your left and head towards a gate in the wall. It's not too obvious and you may well see the sheets of rusted corrugated iron nearby to the right first. Go through the gate and uphill for a short stretch to meet an obvious track which goes left to right.

4. At this point turn right, going through a farm gate, and the valley lies spread out ahead of you. Immediately in front, a large field has two electricity grid pylons. Do not go left with the track towards the plantation but follow the wall downhill and then bear left to go just below the second pylon and through a farm gate. Turn right, and, passing a cottage, go through another gate onto a rutted and muddy farm lane. Ignore the first waymarked gate and continue around the bends to cross a stile on the left just before a couple of houses. From this point you may just see the next ladder stile, half right, where the brook disappears from view. The public right of way goes more or less directly to this point but, unfortunately, an electrified fence is in the way. You will need to go along the fence, and then follow the brook to the right to the next stile. Follow the arrow left to a step stile and then diagonally right to a gate near a telegraph pole. You are now directly above the town and must go to the bottom left corner of the field where a tight walled squeeze next to the cottage leads to the road at Townfoot, which is on the left at the bridge over the burn.

5. This is a good alternative start point, and also a quick way back to the town centre if required. It is, however, also the last section of the walk as described, so cross the bridge and take the first narrow tarmac lane a few metres up on the right. It is not signposted in any way, but leads past a few houses and a white footbridge (off to the right) before dog-legging around a house and field where it changes into a typical riverside footpath. We pass another footbridge, but do not cross it, and then playing fields on the left before arriving back at the tarmac road where we go back to the start via Willea Road.

3   Broomhouse & Bellister

This is an excellent short walk over mixed ground. The Bellister estate has some fine woodland to tramp through, with a glimpse of the old castle through the trees well worthwhile. The section over the moor is quite pleasant, certainly not a slog, although if the mist is down consider choosing another walk! Several variations to the route exist, including shortcuts if required. The walk is described from Burnfoot Farm, although the railway station at Haltwhistle and Park Village would be equally suitable as start points.

Distance	3³/₄ miles(6km)from Burnfoot, 5 miles(8km) from Haltwhistle Railway Station
Time	2-2¹/₂ hrs. 2¹/₂ -3hrs.
Ascent	600 ft.(180m).
Maps	Landranger 87, Pathfinder 546(NY66/76)
Start	Park Burnfoot Farm. GR.684620 From the west end of Haltwhistle take the A689 over the river bridge. Turn right and after a further 1¹/₂ miles, where the road turns sharp left, take the right hand junction to a convenient pull- in opposite the farm. **or** Haltwhistle Railway Station, GR, NY704638

1.   From the roadside park, just opposite Burnfoot farm, walk back up the hill for 50 metres, and just after the entrance to the camp site a stile on the left hand side gives access into the stretch of woodland now under the protection of the National Trust. The path is well worn and easy to follow, but comes very close to the almost vertical drop created where the South Tyne has cut into the valley side. After about fifteen minutes a short clearing with a stile at both ends is reached. As we re-enter the woodland the path twists and turns and then climbs slightly, passing a couple of handy bench seats. Ignore the

stile and path which cuts back sharply to the right. Again the incised meander of the South Tyne creates a steep wooded slope on our left. Although the path appears safe, there are at least two places where the drop is considerable, and care is needed. After the last bench seat the path bears left and then down to the roadside where a wicket gate on either side of the road gives entry to the National Trust woodland which surrounds Bellister Castle.

Bellister Castle - the new house

2. Pleasant footpaths along sloping ground lead past the castle on the left. The modern section is rather large and impressive, while the old is much smaller and partly concealed behind the trees.Continue through the woods, climbing sharply upwards to a stile leading into the open pasture beyond. Go straight up the grassy hill until a solitary marker post is reached, and behind this a large stile next to a metal gate. This is the point at which those starting from Haltwhistle would join the route

3. Ahead Broomhouse Common rises at an easy angle. Nowhere is the going steep or difficult, although when the mist sets in things do become a little featureless. Off on the right the distinctive rough track from Broomhouse Farm makes its way up the moor- our route joins it

after about ten minutes walk. From the stile go across the next field and down to the disused railway line. Continue directly up the hill on the other side and then slightly right to another stile. From this point it is about twenty minutes walk to the farm at Lynnshield, so continue over the wall, moving slightly right, across a field strewn with boulders, to join the wide track coming in from the right. There is a marker post to look for and just to the right of track a rectangular ancient camp. Continue over the rise and down towards a shallow valley. The rough track on the other side of the beck goes straight up the moor and so do we. As a guide our line should be roughly midway between the two walls which lie about two hundred metres either side of us. The wooded summit of Watch Hill on our left, and a ruin with clumps of trees on the right are good pointers because when we draw level with them, just as we descend into the next shallow valley, we must bear slightly right towards a stile and marker post. If in doubt, gradually converge with the wall on the right.

4.   Once over the stile continue along in the same general direction, following a path which can be seen without too much difficulty. A marker post followed by an open gate lead to the farm at Lynnshield. Curve right to the front of the farmhouse which has lovely views overlooking the steep sided dene of Park Burn, but be careful, the drop on the left could be painful. Just past the farmhouse a black corrugated metal barn has a stile in front of it which leads to a gap between the barns.

5.   If you have time the burn is easily reachable, otherwise go through the gap to the farm lane and turn left. This will take you to the main road where a right turn leads in a few minutes to Park Village. The next signpost that we follow is after Park, so a detour through the village is not only more pleasant, but a lot safer. After rejoining the main road, go past the water treatment works and follow the direction to Burnfoot as given by the finger post. Down some steps, over a footbridge and along a sloping tree ringed pasture. As you go downhill, aim for a point just right of the bridge where a wicket will lead back to the start point.

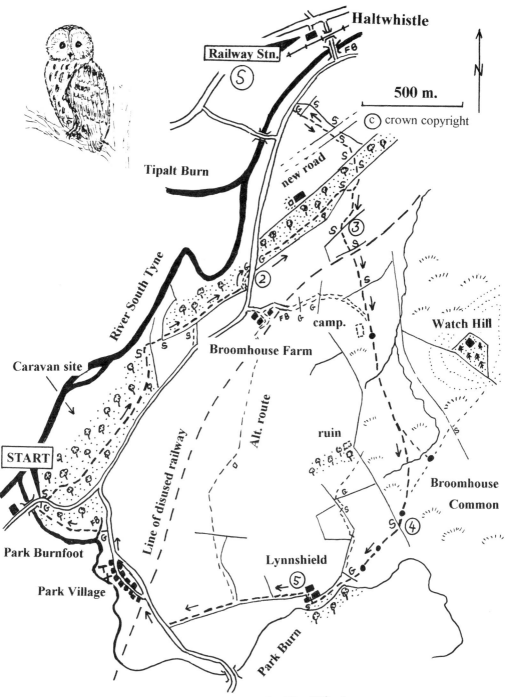

Haltwhistle

Railway Stn.

Ⓢ

500 m.

Ⓒ crown copyright

N

Tipalt Burn

new road

River South Tyne

Caravan site

②

③

FB

Broomhouse Farm

camp.

Watch Hill

Alt. route

ruin

Broomhouse Common

START

Line of disused railway

④

Park Burnfoot

Lynnshield

Park Village

⑤

Park Burn

Broomhouse & Bellister

The bridge at Burnfoot

From HaltwhistleRailway Station, cross the footbridge over the line and follow the ramp down to the left. The river bridge is on the right, and once over it, turn right at the junction along what is known as Bellister road. After a few minutes a gate on the left leads into lush, flat pastures, and the finger post directs the way to Broomhouse Common 1 mile. Cross the pasture towards a strip of woodland. A few stiles on the way suggest work in progress - the Haltwhistle Bypass in fact. The narrow neck of woodland is quickly crossed, and the open pasture continues beyond. The slope is gentle, and if you go half right you will soon reach a marker post and then a large wall stile from which Broomhouse Common is visible. This is point 3 on the route described above.

4   Cawfields, Walltown and Great Chesters

From the recently built picnic and parking site at Cawfields, this super walk takes in a section of the finest 'Wall' country. West bound via Great Chesters and Walltown, following Hadrians Wall as it ascends Mucklebank Crags, through two of the 'nicks' and returning on the level farm lanes which parallel the Whinsill at a lower level.

Distance	4 miles($6^1/_2$km)
Time	allow 2 - 3 hours
Ascent	500 feet.(150m) Including the 'Nicks'.
Maps	Landranger 87, Pathfinder 546(NY66/76)
Start	The Cawfields carpark, GR. 713666

1.   From the carpark move back down the road towards the stone bridge on the right. The finger post on the opposite left-hand side directs us into the field behind Burnhead Cottage and thence to Great Chesters, where you can see the remains of the Roman fort complete with vaulted strongroom. The walk up to the fort is easy angled, keeping to the right hand side of the pleasantly undulating fields, with several prominent stiles. The third of these leads directly to the east side of the fort where the path goes directly through the middle of the rectangle, passing the arched entrance to the strongroom.

The farm at Great Chesters

2.   After passing the vault we exit
through a gap in the western wall,
previously the West Gate, and
head on towards Cockmount
Hill. Looking back provides
a good view of the
prominent outline of the
Whinsill stretching into
the distance. The going
is easy and we soon
gain height, but at this
stage the view to the south
is still impeded by the small

Vaulted arch at Great Chesters

ridge nearby. The house at Cockmount Hill is sheltered from the
prevailing winds by woodland and the path winds its way pleasantly
through a mixture of Spruce on the right and old deciduous woodland
on the left. Five minutes will see you through the trees and on your
way up towards Mucklebank Crags which reach 860'. The climb
steepens somewhat, as expected, but the position is excellent and the
small ridge previously mentioned is now well below us. Much nearer
at hand, probably less than 100 yards away on the left, the line of the
Roman Military Way stands out clearly, less subject to the ups and
downs which our path tends to follow. Route finding is not a
problem, with good paths and stiles to point the way. Descending to
the west of Mucklebank we approach the first 'nick'. Down to the
stile in the bottom,then following the path as it zigzags slightly right
up the steep but fairly short mound. More pleasant meanders along
the ridge, separated by another 'nick', until we finally descend past
the remains of the tiny turret 44B which, because of its aspect, offers
quite comprehensive views to the north and north-west. On a
reasonable day the Solway is not too difficult to see, nor the
prominent hill at Criffell some miles away to the west. The descent
to Walltown is quite steep, but soon leads to a stile and then a farm
track.
3.   This is Walltown Nick. Nearby, quite close to the present

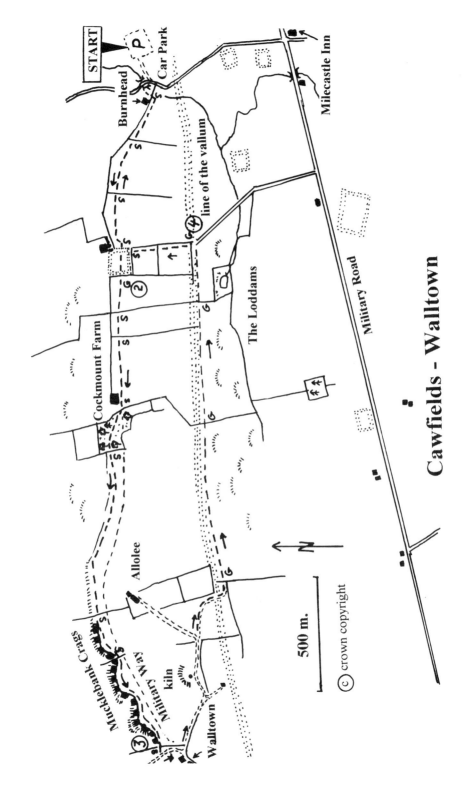

START

Car Park

Burnhead

Milecastle Inn

line of the vallum

④

②

Cockmount Farm

The Loddams

Military Road

Allolee

Mucklebank Crags

Military Way

kiln

Walltown

③

N

500 m.

ⓒ crown copyright

Cawfields - Walltown

Walltown Farm, lies the ancient home of the Ridleys. Today, nothing remains of the house which they had here, but at one time they must have owned half of the area. Turn left and head down to the tarmac lane. The farmhouse is over on the right. Turn left and follow the lane which is almost perfectly flat. Very soon, on the left, we pass a broken down lime kiln complete with its own quarry directly above it. An interesting carved stone gatepost, long since out of service, lies by the wayside.

Lime kiln near Walltown

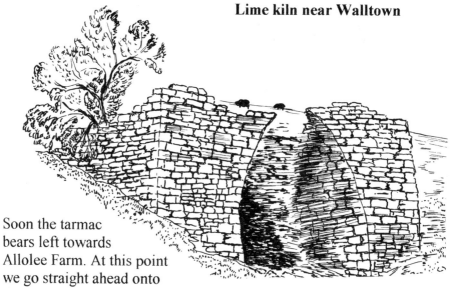

Soon the tarmac bears left towards Allolee Farm. At this point we go straight ahead onto the gravel lane, shortly bearing right to cross a mini ridge and then along one of the best sections of the Vallum. The track is fairly uneventful although as we are paralleling our outward journey the ridge is clearly visible and it is possible to pick out the route taken along the 'wall'. Allolee stands out clearly, as does Cockmount with its protective cloak of woodland to the left and the rows of cultivation terraces below it. The lane becomes tarmac again, and approaching rough pasture ahead it starts to bear right. At this point go left through the gate and along the permissive footpath which lead in five minutes to Great Chesters. Turn right here and retrace the route back down to Cawfields.

5   Cawfields & the Milecastle

Short, easy-going and almost on the level, this most pleasant stroll follows a triangular route between Hadrians Wall and the Milecastle Inn. The start point can be at the Cawfields picnic site or perhaps from the Inn itself.

Distance	2$\frac{1}{2}$ miles(4km.)
Time	Allow 1 hour
Ascent	250ft.(70m)
Maps	Pathfinder 546 (NY66/76)
Start	Cawfields Picnic Site. (GR 713666) Turn off the Military Road at the Milecastle Inn and follow the signs, going north towards the 'Wall' along a narrow country lane.

---

1.   What an unusual setting to begin the walk! The truncated section of the Whinsill sits majestically above the lake which was formed from old quarry workings. The path along the lakeside is followed to Hole gap where a gate on the right provides access to the open ground along the flanks of the Whinsill. Continue slightly uphill, past milecastle 42, and follow the 'wall' along the ridge where you will be rewarded with good views in all directions. (If you prefer a slight diversion, a path also leads to the top of the quarried section). After about twenty minutes walking along the top of CawfieldCrags, cross the stile onto the tarmac lane which goes through Caw gap.

2.   Follow the lane downhill to the right until level with the farm. Going past a double bend, a stile and signpost on the right direct you diagonally left across the moorland. There are tracks of sorts, but nothing worth looking for! You should catch a glimpse of 'Milestone House' situated on the Military Road on the far side of what could be described as 'craglets'. You need to keep to the right of this line of low crags, formerly stone workings, gradually closing with the

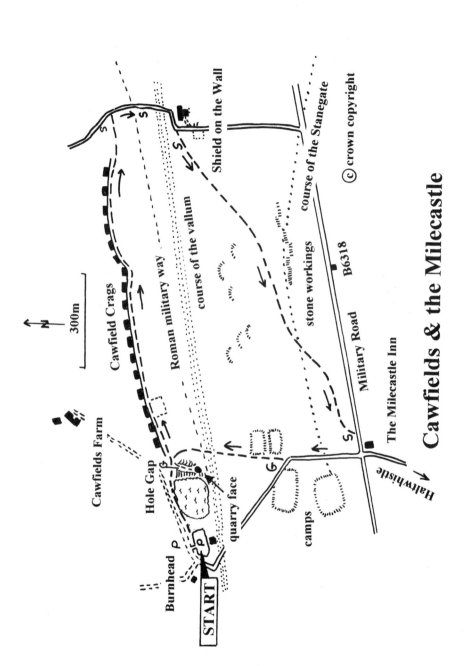

Cawfields & the Milecastle

N

300m

Cawfield Crags

Roman military way

course of the vallum

Shield on the Wall

course of the Stanegate

© crown copyright

stone workings

B6318

Military Road

The Milecastle Inn

Haltwhistle

camps

quarry face

Hole Gap

Cawfields Farm

Burnhead

P

START

S

S

S

S

Military Road where a stile leads you directly to the Milecastle Inn.

The Milecastle Inn

3.   If a stop is desirable, this is the place, but crossing the road needs care. If pressing on back to the carpark, take the lane to the right and follow it as far as a gate on the right where the road bends. This is a short pleasant section which crosses the line of the Vallum and the Roman Military Way before arriving below Milecastle 42 where a left turn will lead back to the Cawfields picnic site.

6   Windshields Crags

Follow Hadrians Wall along one of the high points of the Whinsill and be rewarded with fabulous views. The return leg is via easy angled rough pasture and a quiet country lane.

Distance	3miles(5km)
Time	$1^1/_2$-2hrs.
Ascent	500ft(150m)
Maps	Landranger 87, Pathfinder 546(NY66/76)
Caution	Sadly it is necessary to restate the warnings that thefts have occurred in some of the carparks in the area.
Start	Steel Rigg carpark, which lies about two minutes, by car, north of the Once Brewed visitor Centre. NY751677

---

1. Leaving the carpark, turn left and then right to go over a stile. This is directly on the line of the wall and you will see an explanation board detailing the position of turret 39B, now long gone. The line of the field wall is followed, via two gates, to the summit of Windshield Crags which, at over eleven hundred feet, is one of the highest points in these parts. Looking back to the east gives delightful views, with the characteristic outline of Peel Crag in the near distance being repeated many times as the Great Whinsill dips and rises into the distance. The walk up the slope is fairly easy going, with a couple of walls to give shelter against the westerly winds. Hadrians Wall itself becomes visible half way up, at first only to ankle level but soon assuming more substantial dimensions. To the north, beyond the rolling tracts of Kielder Forest, the rounded mass of Cheviot stands out clearly against the skyline, while to the south the flat topped summit of Cross Fell also stands close to 3000ft.

2. From the trig. point, drop down from the summit in easy steps, still following the ridge, into a nick with a gate and stile at the far

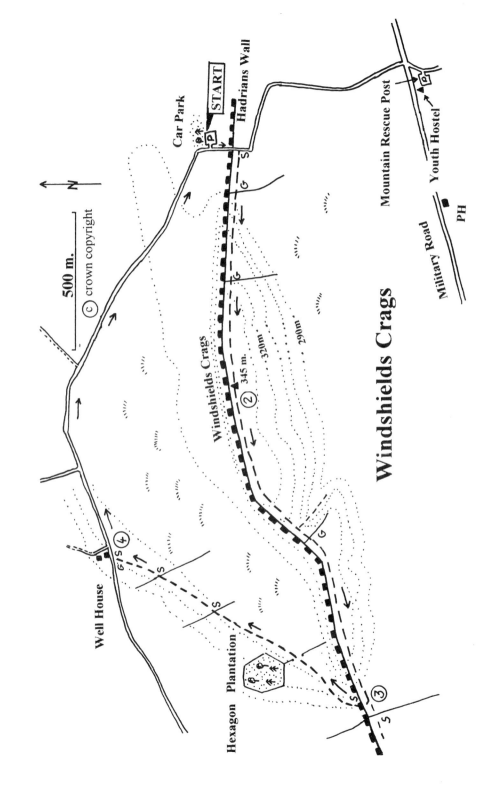

Windshields Crags

START

Car Park

Hadrians Wall

Mountain Rescue Post

Military Road

Youth Hostel

PH

N

500 m.

© crown copyright

Well House

Hexagon   Plantation

Windshields Crags

345 m.

320m

290m

side. This is a sheltered spot, quite often out of the wind in the hollow, and popular with the horses from the local farm. Continue up the other side of the nick and then over the top and down again towards the farm known as Shield on the Wall. Just before reaching this point, a pair of stiles set either side of the wall junction appear.

3.   This walk takes the right hand choice, so, over the wall and into the field beyond. Bear sharp right here, back at an angle, and head towards the right hand side of a pair of copses. The nearest of these to our track, for obvious reasons according to the map, is called Hexagon Plantation. The path is not too distinct, however a solitary gatepost in the first broken down wall, just to the right of the woods is a good aiming point. Continue in the same direction over rough pasture, via two more stiles, heading for a clump of trees next to the farmhouse which is just becoming visible on the other side of a narrow tarmac lane.

4.   Turn right and follow the tarmac back to the carpark. This will take about fifteen minutes, and provide ample time to admire the splendid scenery. If suitably impressed with the views on the left, first of all the shallow valley in which lies Greenlee Lough and then the Whinsill with the weed choked lake beneath the crags, you might not notice the two steepish sections of roadway ahead of you.

7   Steel Rigg Classic

This magnificent short walk starts at the public car park which lies on Steel Rigg, a rounded grassy ridge running parallel to the much more majestic outcrop of whinsill upon which stands Hadrians Wall. Route finding could not be easier! The paths are well marked throughout and follow the excellent farm tracks to the north of the wall via the barns at Peatrigg and Long Side, and then up along the wall itself as it rises and falls along the whinsill with excellent views in all directions. Very popular with visitors, particularly in summer.

Distance	4miles(6$^1/_2$km)
Time	2 - 2$^1/_2$ hours
Ascent	350 ft.(100m) mainly along the wall.
Maps	Landranger 88, Pathfinder 546 (NY 66/76)
Caution	Above Crag Lough the path follows the cliff edge. There is little protection against carelessness, with drops of about 100 feet appearing quite close to the path. Youngsters need **close** supervision.
Start	Steel Rigg Car park, G.R. 751677. From the military road, 3 miles west of Housesteads, turn north at the road junction at Once Brewed National Parks Centre. The parking area lies up the hill on the right.

1.   From the carpark, turn right and follow the road downhill for a few hundred yards. A stile on the righthand side, and a finger post, direct you to Hotbank Farm, which you will soon see is located between Crag Lough and Hotbank Crag some one and a half miles away. The track is firm and wide and will take you to within ten minutes walk of the farm. As you meander along, take a look across to the right, past the rounded ridge. Peel Crag starts to come into

view. First the tops, and gradually, as Steel Rigg tapers away, the full height of the crags become visible. My first introduction to these crags, some thirty years ago, was climbing the numerous vertical cracks formed by the cooling quartze dolerite, a very typical feature of the outcrops along the whinsill. Even before that time groups of climbers had been scaling every conceivable fissure, describing, grading and recording for the benefits of other enthusiasts, not to mention a bit of good old-fashioned competition.

The farm lane climbs imperceptibly, running against the Peatrigg plantation packed with scots pine and birch. Soon the old barn comes into view. A composite building with the old stone section partly hidden by the larger and much rusted corrigated-iron add-on. Even in quite light wind conditions the flapping of the cladding can sometimes be heard before the barn is sighted. Continue along the flat until Long Side Barn is reached.

2.   From this point excellent views across the grassy slopes reveal the whinsill outcrop in all its glory, standing proudly above the waters of the lough. High Shield Crag (known by rock climbers as Crag Lough) and Peel Crag are separated by two little mounds with their associated 'nicks' (Castle Nick is probably the best known), and the excavated and rebuilt sections of the wall can be clearly seen faithfully following the contours of the ups and downs. Continue past the field corner on the left, and cross the stile in the wall ahead of you. The track then goes through a zigzag, across a ditch, and into hayfields. Soon you should see a rough farm track on the other side of the next wall. Cross two stiles at right angles, and follow the track up to the right towards Hotbank Farm nestling between the crags.

3.   The farmyard starts with a metal gate and ends with a stile giving access to the wall itself. This is a very popular section of the wall,

and the short distance between this point and Milking Gap can be quite busy during the summer months. Leaving Hotbank, turn right, going down the hill. On your immediate left is the remains of Milecastle 38. The shape of the Milecastle is indicated by a trench, left after eighteenth century stone raiders had laid it to waste.

4.   On reaching Milking Gap, a stile leads you over the farm wall and the signposts which now confront you, give a confusing choice of direction. Although this walk follows the line of the wall, going along the summits of the whinsill, this is by no means the only way back to your transport. If you want something different it is possible to walk along the broken paths which shadow the base of the cliffs, tracks used by climbers and sheep. Go this way however and you will miss the delights of the walk along the ridge. There is also a very good alternative for bad weather, or perhaps you would just like to avoid the huffing and puffing involved in going up and down the ridge. I refer to the 'Military Way' which can be reached by going left down the lane a matter of yards to the signpost and then following it back to Steel Rigg. This may also save 10-15 minutes.

The normal classic walk goes across the 'Gap' and over the stile which is near the cattle grid. This takes you onto the line of the wall itself, so turn left going uphill at a fairly easy angle until another stile gives access into the thinly scattered woods which crown the top of Crag Lough. The angle remains easy, but we do gain height, albeit slowly. The numerous Scots Pine become sparse, and as we near the top of the ridge, bracken, roughgrass and stunted bushes predominate. Take the opportunity to look across the field wall to the left ! The course of the 'Military Way' can be seen close by, and further over, the fast and furious 'Military Road' which was built by General Wade in the middle of the 18th. century to speed up the movement of troops between east and west. Unfortunately much of the building materials were taken from the 'Wall'. Beyond, on the other side of the valley stands the dark mass of Barcombe Hill, itself also much used in the past to supply quarried materials for the building of Hadrians Wall. The route ahead is obvious, one might almost say inescapable with well made paths and stiles leading us

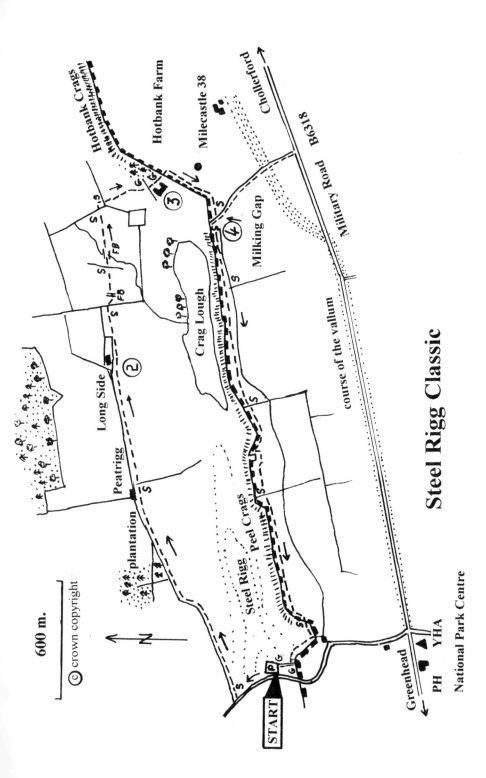

Steel Rigg Classic

600 m.

© crown copyright

N

Hotbank Crags

Hotbank Farm

• Milecastle 38

Chollerford

B6318

Military Road

course of the vallum

Long Side

Peatrigg

plantation

② Crag Lough

③

④ Milking Gap

Steel Rigg

Peel Crags

FB

FB

START

P

Greenhead

PH   YHA

National Park Centre

past rebuilt sections of wall, a milecastle, and a few turrets. There are a couple of steep descents into the 'nicks' so do take care. Walking along the crag tops, the path often comes to within inches of a 100 foot drop. There are few warning signs, and safety is very much a common sense thing. Children need close supervision at all times, particularly in wet and windy conditions.

Looking south towards Peel Crag

The last descent at the end of Peel Crag is most impressive. It starts with a stile and then a series of stone steps which pick out a sensible route, eventually following a line of slabs across the boggy ground adjacent to a new looking section of the wall. Continue up the hill, keeping to the path which finally delivers us, via two gates, back to Steel Rigg.

Vindolanda, Housesteads & 'The Wall'

Three of the most important features of the Roman presence in Northumberland are visited on this route. Enjoy the spectacular walk along the wall between Housesteads and Milking Gap.

Distance	5½ miles(9km)
Time	allow $2^1/_2$-$3^1/_2$ hours
Ascent	500 ft.(150m) undulating
Maps	Landranger 87, Pathfinder 546 (NY66/76)
Caution	Steep drop to the north side of the Wall. Take care in windy or icy conditions.
Start	Vindolanda carpark. Arriving at Bardon Mill bypass, leave the A69 at a minor road which is signposted *Once Brewed and Hadrian's Wall*. As you approach Once Brewed, for a long time a youth hostel and now also a National Park Information Centre, a signpost directs you to Vindolanda. If you are arriving via the Military Road, turn South at the Once Brewed and after ½ mile, left again - the sign will direct you. GR.NY769664. eastern park GR. NY774665

---

1. Leave the Western car park of Vindolanda and entering the lane which follows Stanegate, turn right and walk downhill into the dene of Bradley Burn and the entrance to Chesterholme, which is guarded by two white lionheads.

If you look past the stile on your left a large Roman Milestone, almost circular in section, stands about 5½ feet high. Numerous different miles exist, but this Roman one was approximately 1620 yards. Continue up the hill as the lane bears right. It would have been nice to stop at Chesterholme for refreshments, but we've only just started so why not keep that for the end of the walk, while looking around Vindolanda. At the top of the lane a **T** junction, below the mass of Barcombe Hill, marks a temporary end to the uphill plod. Barcombe Hill was used by the Romans for the extraction of building blocks for the wall, and also, because of its prominence, as a signalling station. An Iron Age settlement at the Northern end testifies to its earlier occupation. Turn left along the shallow incline to a road junction.

2. Although the road bears right here, only two minutes away, down the lane to the left, you will find the Crindledyke Lime Kiln. At one time there would have been upto 300 of these kilns in the county, although this may have been the only one with four arched flues (two of which could be closed down when necessary). The ramp visible at the back was used to trundle the limestone and coal up to the top for tipping in.

Continuing this walk, from the junction, go along the road bearing right, over the crest and turn left at the farm track to East Crindledykes. Pass the farm on your left, through the edge of the yard and into the pasture. Follow the rutted track across the two mini escarpments, down into a dip and then up to a ladder stile giving access to the fast and furious Military Road. This was built by General Wade in the 1750's to facilitate troop movements across country. Unfortunately, as it follows the line of Hadrian's Wall much of the raw materials were taken from the Wall itself.

3. On the opposite side of the road, slightly right, a farm gate gives access to a lane which goes up to Housesteads farm, the Fort and Visitors Centre. Pass the farm and office on your left, then go up the left hand side of the fort to its north western corner, where you will find a stile giving access onto the wall. Take advantage of the view. It is easy to appreciate the fortified nature of Housesteads and the Wall just by looking at the vertical nature of the Whinsill outcrop upon which you now stand. At one time upto 1000 men would have been stationed here, ensuring a thriving civilian population, or, vicus, in the vicinity. It is said to be the best preserved fort on the Wall, and although it dates from A.D.128 when it was constructed to defend against invasion along the Knag Burn, most of the remains that are visible now date much later during the third or fourth century AD.

4. No route finding problems for the next stage! Turn left and follow the wall, initially actually walking on it, going up and down a few crests. Eventually you will pass Hotbank Farm on your right and then the trench of Milecastle 38, another victim of stone raiders looking for building materials.

5. We are descending now into Milking gap, and a sign points us in the direction of a rough lane. What a plethora of signs! Today we don't need them, but turn left down the lane, going past the Military Way PFS, until after a few minutes we see a sign which we do need, since it directs us back to Vindolanda 1¼ miles, via High Shield ½ mile. This direction takes us across boggy land, across the line of the Vallum and on to a ladder stile in the far corner of the field, and then another to our left, leading to the Military road near High Shield Farm.

6. Cross the road and go down the farm lane, where a stile on the left leads into a pasture. Circumnavigate what was a barn, and is now a new house, on your right, bearing right, and then head straight down the left hand side of two large fields. A sign post and stile start you off, then another stile halfway down. Where the field boundary ends, keep going in the same direction, then bearing right into the wooded area of Bradley Burn. Soon you will see the old milestone and a stile leading into the Stanegate. Turn right, and change into

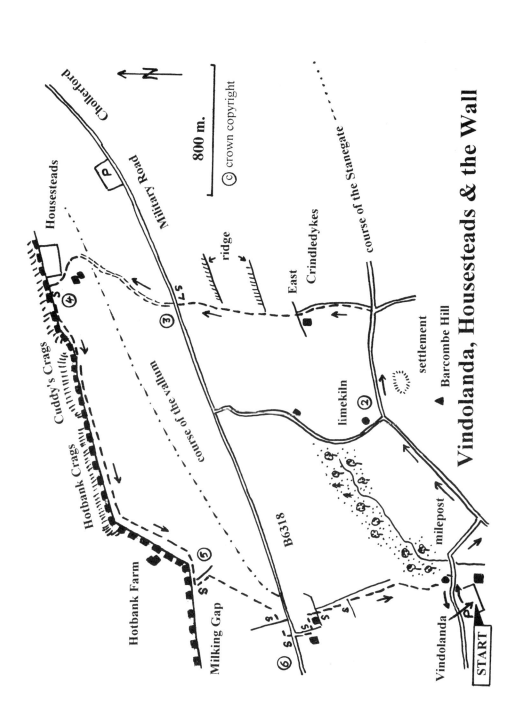

Vindolanda, Housesteads & the Wall

Chollerford

Housesteads

P

Military Road

N

800 m.

© crown copyright

ridge

East
Crindledykes

course of the Stanegate

Cuddy's Crags

Hotbank Crags

course of the vallum

settlement

▲ Barcombe Hill

limekiln

②

Hotbank Farm

B6318

milepost

Milking Gap

⑤

⑥

⑥

③

④

Vindolanda

P

START

low gear for the walk up to your car.

It would be a great shame not to have a look around Vindolanda. It was built as part of the Stanegate frontier system from A.D.90 onwards. Several forts were built, the earlier ones of wood, but the remains seen now, like those at Housesteads, are dated much later into the third century. The reconstruction is well worth a look.

Reconstruction at Vindolanda

9   Chineley Burn and Barcombe Hill

An easy stroll down the burn, followed by the pleasant drag up Barcombe Hill and the reward of splendid views all round make this a very rewarding route. Like the Haltwhistle Burn, further west, this burn provided power for small woollen mills which operated from the late 18th. century and was also the site of coal mining which continued until quite recently.

Distance	3½ miles(5³/₄km)
Time	allow 2 - 2½ hours
Ascent	600 ft.(180m), mainly the walk up Barcombe Hill
Maps	Landranger 87, Pathfinder 546 (NY66/76)
Start	Vindolanda carpark. Arriving at Bardon Mill bypass, leave the A69 at a minor road which is signposted *Once Brewed and Hadrian's Wall*. As you approach Once Brewed, for a long time a youth hostel and now also a National Park Information Centre, a signpost directs you to Vindolanda. If you are arriving via the Military Road, turn South at the Once Brewed and follow the signs GR. NY769664

1.   Leave the Western car park of Vindolanda and entering the lane which follows Stanegate, turn right and walk downhill into the dene of Bradley Burn and the entrance to Chesterholme, which is guarded by two white lionheads. Turn right and go down the museum drive, between the buildings, and look for the yellow markers. If you keep on the main track, avoiding the fork which splits off left, you will border the gardens of Chesterholme where some of the museum relics and reconstructions are clearly visible. The land on both sides is private and to begin with we are constrained to the footpath, but after a footbridge and several stiles the walk opens out a little as it follows the west bank of the burn. The gentle slopes are very pleasant

and the walking could not be easier. Soon the cottage at Low Fogrigg comes into view, sitting next to an almost dried up river bed and a wooden bridge. The track now becomes gravel, staying fairly high above the steepening slopes on the left. Avoid being suckered into a likely looking path which goes meaningfully down towards the stream. It's a dead end ! So, staying at the same level, go past gates and stiles until you reach four large concrete blocks near the overhead power lines. On the way to this point it would be difficult to miss the distinctive black scars left by mining waste on the other side of the burn. Bear right to pass between the first two pylons and across the field to a gate in the corner. Beyond lies the tarmac road which is followed downhill to the left.

2.   While walking down the road take a look across to the left. The row of old cottages known as Westwood is the point that we're heading for, but of course we have to loop round the road to do this, so turn left at the junction and slog up the hill past a telephone box on the left and then a mailbox set in the wall. Turn right and after passing the cottages, a strategically placed seat on the left is all the encouragement needed to view the countryside to the South.

3.   This is the start of the gentle climb up Barcombe Hill. The stile nearby leads into a field which has an obvious track going up to the side of the farm at West End Town. If you keep to the right of the trees several breaks in the wall lead into an enclosed farm track. Turn right to go in front of the farm house, through a small metal gate and then left up a walled lane. After five minutes, a stile and signpost leading to Thorngrafton Common presents a choice of routes.

4.   The Thorngrafton variation is easier going, but longer, and misses out on the splendid views in all directions which we can get from Barcombe Hill. So, let us ignore the stile. Continue up the lane, over a different stile, and pick up the well worn track where the walls end and the moor begins. This bit of heathland was walled off during the 'enclosures' some 200 years ago, although today there are several paths which can be followed upto the ridge which runs along Barcombe Hill. The well worn path ahead zigzags us up in easy stages to the right of the woods and then, passing an area of broken

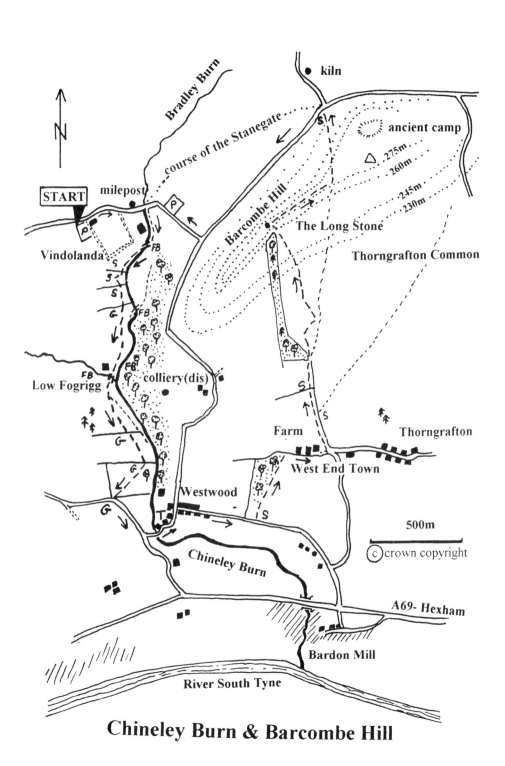

Chineley Burn & Barcombe Hill

wall, quite suddenly, nothing at all. We are on the ridge fairly close to the Long Stone, a prominent finger of rock which was once the site of a Roman signalling station, and very convenient for todays wanderers because it can be seen without difficulty from the bottom of the moor.

Chesterholme

5.   The ridge line is perfect ! Unless the visibility has deteriorated this is the place to get the best of views, and if it is time for a break there are a couple of excellent picnic spots. They are well sheltered from the prevailing wind, and being on the northern edge of the ridge give excellent panoramic views of Hadrians Wall country. The ridge stretches eastwards towards the summit. As this point is approached a well used track crosses at right angles. This is in fact one of the rights of way which goes down to the foot of the moor on the right. We could have taken this route, but in doing so would have missed out on the ridge. Two minutes away, on the other side of the summit, should you wish to linger, the outlines of an ancient settlement still stand out clearly. At the junction turn left and follow the path down the hill towards the road. Nearby you may see the old lime kiln at Crindledykes, two minutes away on the other side of the road. Once on the tarmac, turn left and after five or ten minutes on the level take the right junction and so on down to Chesterholme.

10 A Walk along 'The Wall' from Housesteads

This superb walk takes in the spectacular views which can be seen from the wall in all directions. The northern section, which passes close to Broomlee Lough, affords fine views of the whole sequence of the Whinsill from King's Hill to Peel Crag, and, perhaps, a fuller appreciation of the military strategic importance of the Whinsill which can only been seen from this direction.

Distance	4½ miles(7km)
Time	allow 2 - 3 hours
Ascent	500 feet(150m)
Maps	Landranger 87, Pathfinder 546(NY66/76)
Caution	The wall passes directly above the vertical drop of the Whinsill which can be 80 feet above the scree below.
Start	The Housesteads carpark is adjacent to the Military Road, B6318, approximately eight miles west of Chollerford. GR.NY794684

1. From the carpark follow the main track up towards the Housesteads fort and museum. The visible remains of the fort are well preserved and date from the third century. Covering about four acres and rectangular in shape, Housesteads is positioned on a slope close to the crest of the Whinsill giving it an ideal defensive position. Pass the fort on its left and go to the north west corner where a stile gives access to the wall itself.
2. From this position, go down slightly and then right below the fortifications above. At this point the wall drops steeply and then curves left to the Knag Burn Gate, the site of frequent invasions from the north which necessitated the building of the fort with a garrison of one thousand men. Cross through the gate and follow uphill on the other side of what is now just a normal wall. Pass through a copse of trees via stiles at both sides, up along the crest of the

Whinsill to King's Hill from where you can look across left to Broomlee Lough. Wark Forest, stretching away to the horizon where it joins up with the vast tracts of coniferous plantations of Kielder Forest, is behind the lough, and together with Kielder makes up over 100,000 acres of spruce and pine. Go down King's Hill and across a stile, or through the gate, on your left, at King's Wicket.

3. From this point the path leads back to the west, not quite parallel to the line of the escarpment, but from here you should see a small stand of trees about 600 metres away. When you reach the woods, a ladder stile at both sides makes the crossing easier. You can go round if you prefer, but it is rather nice meandering through the young Pine trees. Continue in the same general direction, and you will eventually arrive at a large ladder stile which is on the Pennine way. This was the first national trail to be created by what is now known as the Countryside Commission. Opened in 1965, it stretches for about 250 miles from Edale in Derbyshire to Kirk Yetholm just over the Scottish border. To the right the Pennine way continues north between Greenlee and Broomlee Loughs, while to the left it cuts through the Whinsill gap between Hotbank Crags and Cuddy's crags.

Hotbank Farm and Crag lough

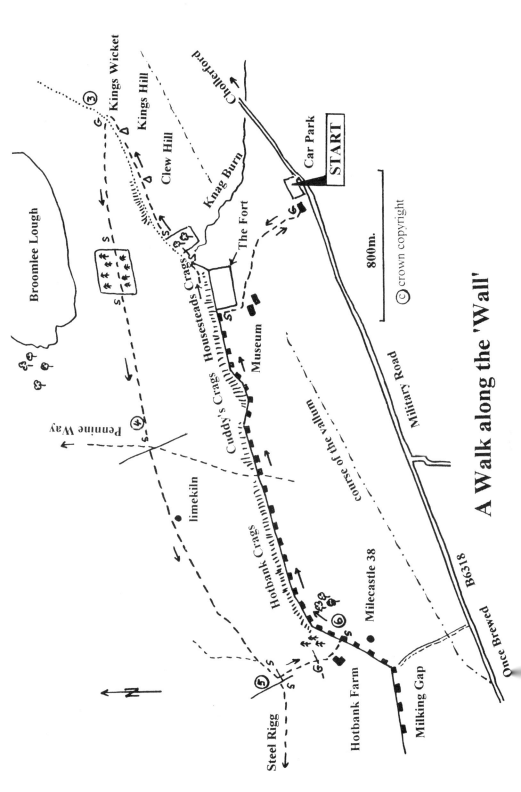

A Walk along the 'Wall'

Broomlee Lough

Kings Wicket

③

Kings Hill

Clew Hill

Knag Burn

Chollerford

Car Park

START

800m.

© crown copyright

The Fort

Housesteads Crags

Museum

course of the vallum

Military Road

Cuddy's Crags

Pennine Way

④

limekiln

Hotbank Crags

Milecastle 38

⑥

Steel Rigg

⑤

Hotbank Farm

Milking Gap

B6318

Once Brewed

N

4.   Over the stile and head for a lime kiln a few hundred paces ahead. The kilns are quite a common feature in Northumberland, being used extensively in the eighteenth and nineteenth centuries for the production of lime to neutralise the acidic soils. Pass the kiln and continue on a broad grassy area down to meet a track converging from the right. Bear left here past a marker post, and take a good look at Crag Lough and Peel Crag ahead of you and on the right. Both have been extensively used by rock climbers for decades now, the vertical cracks and buttresses formed by masses of cooling Quartz Dolerite being ideal for short vertical climbs. Below Crag Lough a tarn of the same name has been formed by the depression left at the end of the last ice age some ten thousand years ago. It is now partly silted up and the reeds which flourish there conceal an abundance of wildfowl.

5.   Continue bearing left on the somewhat muddy track until you arrive at a farm gate complete with ladder stile. To the right another stile, which we ignore, leads to the Steel Rigg carpark. Passing to the left of Hotbank Farm, over another stile and we are back on the Wall.

6.   From here the route is unambiguous, going left along the line of the Wall, up and down the crests, and eventually even upon the Wall itself, until we arrive back at Housesteads and so back down to the carpark.

11   Brocolitia & Simonburn

A mixture of easy going paths along country lanes, over farmland, through wooded denes and along an old drovers road. Although not spectacular like the ridge walks further west, the varied terrain is both peaceful and interesting, with the walk passing Roman remains, a twelfth century church, ancient castle, an old folly, and views of Nunwick Hall and Chipchase Castle. The walk can be covered as a whole, or broken into two smaller sections depending on the desired starting point.

Distance	$5^1/_2$miles(9k) complete walk, $3^3/_4$miles(6km) Brocolitia section, $2^3/_4$miles($4^1/_2$km) Simonburn section .
Time	2-$2^1/_2$hrs, $1^1/_2$-2hrs, 1-$1^1/_2$hrs.
Ascent	800ft.(250m) 650ft.(200m) 500ft.(150m)
Maps	Landranger 87, Pathfinder 534(NY87/97)
Start	Brocolitia carpark on the Military Road,or the small carpark adjacent to Simonburn Church GR. NY871736

1   Turn right out of the official park and make your way up the easy incline towards a turning on the left which will lead to High Teppermoor Farm. The verges are narrow and the road has a false summit at each end of this stretch, so great care is needed if you are to enjoy the rest of the walk. Turn left into the farm lane and cross the stile near the farm buildings. The broken farm track heads off diagonally right towards another stile and then through a gate near a finger of woodland. Continue along the treeline towards a wall where the route bears left towards another stile. From this point the farms at Tecket and Uppertown are just visible, partly concealed by the slope and woodland around Crook Burn. Move half left down the steep and fairly rough ground, and two more stiles and a gate lead into the farmyard of Uppertown.

2.   Just before reaching the farmhouse, when level with an old

overgrown barn, take a sharp turn left and follow a farm track to a small gate into the woods. The path here is fairly steep and slippery in places, and the loose fencing does not leave a lot to hang onto. The foot of the descent is soon reached however, and a wooden bridge takes us across the Crook Burn. At some time in the past the burn must have been a lot more active than today because, although the slopes to the left are reasonably easy angled, further downstream the slopes are rocky and the valley almost gulf like. From the bridge go half left and strike up the valley side towards the left hand side of the farm at Tecket. A gate followed by two stiles along the boundary fence lead to the narrow stretch of tarmac which provides an access road to the outlying farms. If you move left a short distance to a bridge and a cottage you can make a choice as to which route will be followed.

3. The shorter walk goes straight ahead and up the lane, passing a few houses and a farm, to the start of the old drove road, marked as point 4 on the diagram. For the longer walk, which takes in the village of Simonburn, turn right over the bridge and follow the lane gently downhill, paralleling the burn for about fifteen minutes until the village is reached. Simonburn was once the largest parish in the county and today stands as a picturesque village green, with a memorial cross, and surrounded by a scattering of houses. St. Mungo's church is on the left, and rounding the corner the entrance is through a magnificent lych-gate, erected in 1866 in memory of Lancelot Allgood of Nunwick. There is a good carpark at the side of the church and so this would be a good alternative start point if required. Continue across the front of the church and up the lane towards the post office at which point our lane bears left and then down to the bridge over the Hopeshield Burn. There are several tracks here! We bear left and follow the concrete access road which climbs above and alongside the burn, passing the well ruined Simonburn Castle. Originally built by the Herons of Chipchase to station one hundred men, and rebuilt as a folly in the eighteenth century, it is now little more than a mound with one wall and a couple of arched doors or windows. Continue up the road, leaving

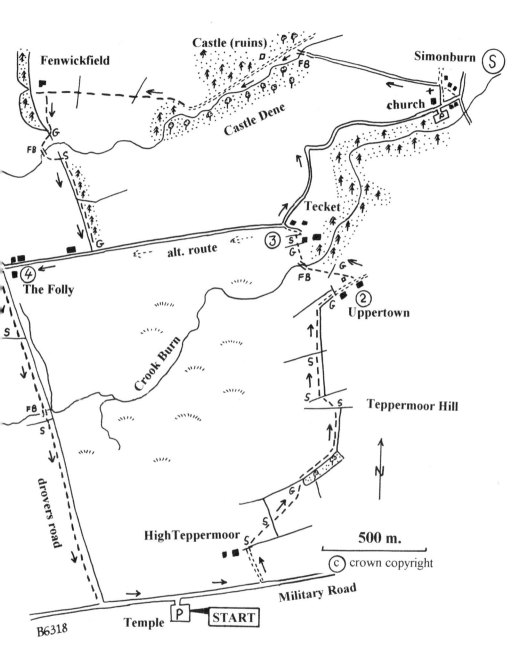

Brocolitia & Simonburn

the woodland behind and entering an area of open pasture, not unlike an alpine meadow in summer. When level with the farm known as Fenwickfield, the right of way goes left and down to the bottom of the finger of woodland. There is a path running alongside the treeline, however, and this may be more suitable with animals or crops in the field. Where the trees thin out at the bottom of the slope a small gate on the right gives access to a footbridge over the burn. This is followed immediately by a stile which enables you to return to the left hand side of the boundary. Turn right and go up the hill, through two gates, along the edge of another finger of woodland. The right of way seems to sit on the fence here, but the only visible track, and the position of the gates, suggests that the woods may be the best option. When you reach the lane, turn right and walk to the end of the road next to the house known as Kirkshield. This was built by a rector of Simonburn for use as a hunting lodge and has a most unusual profile.

Kirkshield - the folly

4.   The end of the road is crossed by an old drovers road which runs in a straight line directly back to the military road, so turn left and follow the wide green lane downhill to a footbridge, then up the gradual slope, passing a few stiles on the way, until you reach the tarmac. Turn left and then back to the carpark where details of local Roman history is displayed on a board.

12   Fallowfield Fell

A combination of farmland tracks, wooded denes,open grassland and narrow unfenced country lanes make this a pleasant varied walk with very little ascent. Not as spectacular as the walks further west, but well worth doing.

Distance	3miles(5km)
Time	$1^{1/}_{2}$ - 2 hours
Ascent	250ft.(80m)
Maps	Landranger 87, Pathfinder 547 (NY86/96)
Caution	Take care when wandering up the dene
Start	Layby at St. Oswalds, just over one mile east of the crossroads at Chollerford (where the Hexham road crosses the Military Road). GR. NY937694

At one end of the layby, a large wooden cross erected in the 1930's commemorates the battle of Heavenfield, fought between the armies of Cadwallon and Oswald in 635AD. The original cross was sited on the slight rise of ground to the north which has been occupied by the church of St. Oswald since 1737.

On this site originally, a small church had been built in honour of Oswald who, according to Bede, brought the Christian faith to an area which previously had none.

1.   Cross the road and follow the narrow lane past St. Oswalds Cottage, down the dip and up the other side. The hollow which has just been passed is marked on the map as Mould's Close, and is said to have been where the fiercest of fighting took place. Remnants of weapons and skulls, remains of the two armies, have been found in profusion here. The defeated leader, Cadwallon, escaped southwards, but was caught and killed only a few miles to the south on the banks of the Rowley Burn. Once up the slope a metal gate gives access to a

wide expanse of open grassland. Whereas the tarmac lane goes right towards the farm at Fallowfield, our route goes directly across the field towards the right hand edge of a stand of trees known appropriately enough as SquareWood. The soil depth is shallow here and as we cross the field, going past old quarry workings, the rock pavement has been exposed where the turf has been worn away. Approaching the trees, bear right towards a wooden gate at the bottom corner of the field. Ahead lies the Tyne valley with the small settlement of Acomb nestling comfortably at the bottom of the hill.

2   Turn left here and follow the farm track, quite rutted and muddy in places, past another two large wooden gates, and descending slightly towards the wooded dene ahead. The caravan site comes into view between the trees on the right and very soon a gate next to an old ruined barn provides access into what turns out to be quite a broken area of trees, scrub and mining remains.

Mining Relics

After going a few paces into the woods, turn left at a wooden marker post and follow the course of the dene. The way should be fairly obvious, even though the path winds tortuously though the brush and scattered trees, going imperceptibly upwards and past a couple of tiny footbridges. At one point the path goes directly over a three pot limekiln, and the short scramble down the slope to the left, to get a better view, is well worth the effort.

3 You will eventually leave this narrow little valley just below the

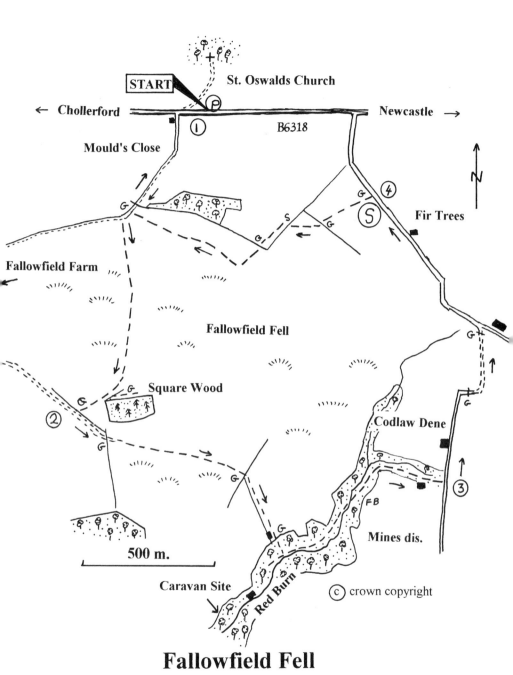

Fallowfield Fell

farm known as Codlaw Dene. Turn left at the roadway and make your way uphill past the farm which is complete with its pigeon house fixed half way up the gable end of the building. The lane goes easily onwards through a zigzag and bears left at the next farm, Codlaw Hill. The going is still easy, and the views of the valley are very pleasant. The next house on the right, Fir trees, is passed, and shortly a gate on the left leads into a large flat pasture.

4   Cross the pasture towards a field gate after which a right turn leads, across a complex area of horse jumps, towards a large stile over the stone wall. Bearing left, a small gate leads onto the open rough pasture. Walk ahead for a short distance and then bear right to parallel the field wall, climbing slightly across the rock pavement to arrive at the metal gate above Mould's Close and then back along the lane to the Layby.

Church of St. Oswald